# Contents

KU-506-938

# Tornadoes

Kathy Galashan

Published in association with The Basic Skills Agency

Hodder & Stoughton
A MEMBER OF THE HODDER HEADLINE GROUP

**Acknowledgements**

Cover: Steve Bloom/Telegraph Colour Library

Photos: pp 2, 14, 22 Popperfoto/Reuters; p 5 Planet Earth Pictures;
p 18 Steve Bloom/Telegraph Colour Library

Illustration: Maureen Carter

Every effort has been made to trace copyright holders of material reproduced in this book. Any rights not acknowledged will be acknowledged in subsequent printings if notice is given to the publisher.

Orders; please contact Bookpoint Ltd, 39 Milton Park, Abingdon, Oxon OX14 4TD. Telephone: (44) 01235 400414, Fax: (44) 01235 400454. Lines are open from 9.00–6.00, Monday to Saturday, with a 24 hour message answering service.
Email address: orders@bookpoint.co.uk

*British Library Cataloguing in Publication Data*
A catalogue record for this title is available from the British Library

ISBN  0 340 77522 X

First published  2000
Impression number   10 9 8 7 6 5 4 3 2 1
Year                2005 2004 2003 2002 2001 2000

Copyright © 2000  Kathy Galashan

Typeset by GreenGate Publishing Services, Tonbridge, Kent.
Printed in Great Britain for Hodder and Stoughton Educational, a division of Hodder Headline Plc, 338 Euston Road, London NW1 3BH, by Redwood Books, Trowbridge, Wilts

# 1  Joe's Story

Joe is a policeman.
He lived through a tornado.

This is his story.

'I was at work.
I was driving a patrol car.
It was 4pm.

First I saw small white clouds.
Then I saw dark clouds.
In seconds the tornado was there,
in front of me.
It looked like
an upside-down Christmas tree.

Lights were flashing inside,
blue and white.
There was lightning and blue flashes
as the tornado hit power lines.
It was very frightening
but very beautiful.

I was in shock.

A tornado is very frightening.

The air in front was thick with flying rubbish.
I saw a shoe, letters, all sorts of things.
People's lives were flying around
in the air.

The path of the tornado
headed for the middle of town.
My house, my wife, my child were there.
Were they alive or dead?

I drove to my house,
past people screaming
and hurt.
The house was gone.

An hour later, I found my wife, Jean.
It was the longest hour of my life.'

## 2  Jean's Story

'I heard the sirens.
The tornado was coming.
I grabbed the baby.
I ran into a room
in the middle of the house.

I got on my knees
under a large wooden table.
I put pillows by my back.
I put my head between my knees
and a duvet over my head.
I held the baby tight.
I prayed.

Sheltering from a tornado.

The roof blew off the house.
The noise was tremendous.
There was a rush of air.
It sucked me out.
It felt like my brains
were coming through my ears.
I thought I was dying.

Then it was over, quiet.
I pushed away wood and rubbish
and crawled out.
The baby and I were safe.
The house was flattened.

A week later, I found my jewellery box.
It belonged to my grandmother
and was very special.
It was half a mile away
and the jewellery was still inside.'

# 3  What is a Tornado?

A tornado is a funnel of air
spinning round and round.
In the middle of the funnel
it is really quiet.
Sometimes tornadoes are called twisters.

A tornado starts when warm air
meets cold air.
The warm air is pushed up
as high as 40,000 feet.
This makes storms.
The winds in the top part of the cloud
can start the air spinning.

The winds get faster.
The clouds become shaped
like a funnel.
At the bottom of the cloud
air gets sucked in.
The funnel reaches
down to the ground.
A tornado is born.

Tornadoes spin clockwise
south of the equator.
They spin anticlockwise
north of the equator.

# 4  Where do Tornadoes Happen?

Tornadoes always start over land.
They can happen almost
anywhere in the world.

In July 1999 a tornado was spotted
in Scotland by a Tornado jet.

In some places they are very common.
The midwest of the USA
is known as Tornado Alley.
About 700 tornadoes a year
are reported.

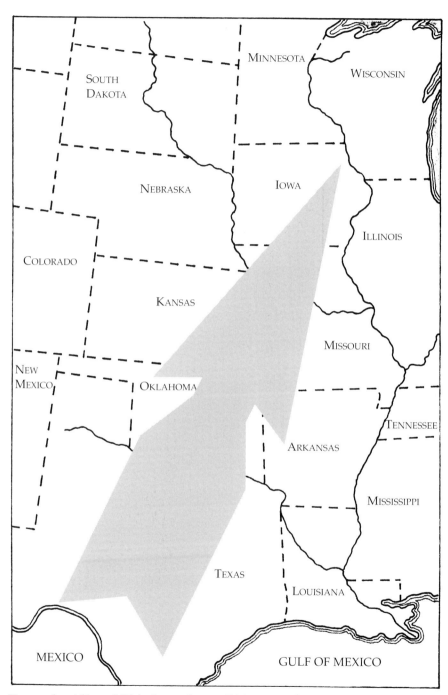

Tornado Alley, USA, has about 700 tornadoes a year.

On 3 May 1999, 50 tornadoes
passed through Oklahoma in 8 hours.
45 people died.
Thousands were injured.
An area 1 mile wide
and 38 miles long
was turned into rubble.

The tornado season is April to June.
Most happen in the afternoon or evening.

# 5 Signs of a Tornado

- Stormy weather.
  There may be hailstones.
  There may be lightening.

- The clouds may look greenish or greenish black.
  Clouds are spinning.
  Sometimes they are funnel-shaped.

- There may be a wall of cloud
  just above the ground.

- Animals and pets are jumpy.
  They seem to know when a tornado is coming.

- There is a rushing sound
  that turns into a roar.

# 6  Tornado Chasers

Some people go looking for tornadoes.
Some do it for fun.
For some it is a job.
They film tornadoes
and sell pictures to TV.

Some work for weather centres
and universities.
They film and collect information.
People can even book
a tornado chaser holiday.

Tornadoes are not big.
They are usually
much less than half a mile across.
It's easy to miss one.

Chasers have to be
in the right place
at the right time.

Chasers filming a tornado.

It can be dangerous
following a tornado.
The driving is difficult.
Filming a video on the move
is difficult.

Strong winds can push
the car around.
It's dark and lightning is flashing.

The rain is heavy, very heavy.
Hail can cause a lot of damage.
Hail the size of golf balls
can smash a windscreen.

People chase tornadoes
because they are beautiful
and exciting.
But they are not easy to find.
It's hard to know when or where
a tornado will start.

Chasers study weather forecasts.
They study the weather.
They know the signs.
They make guesses.
They drive long distances.
Sometimes they are lucky.

# 7 Predicting a Tornado

People need to know
when a tornado is coming.

Chasers send in reports.
TV and radio warn people
of tornadoes.
In Tornado Alley,
there are even weather updates
at petrol stations.

The swirling funnel-shaped cloud of a tornado.

A Tornado Watch tells people
to listen to reports.
A Tornado Warning tells people
there is a tornado on the ground.
There may be a funnel-shaped cloud coming.
Sirens go off.
People take cover.

If too many warnings are wrong,
there are problems.
People can waste hours
hiding against a tornado.
People stop listening to warnings.
Then when the big one hits,
it's too late.

# 8 What to do in a Tornado

The best place to be is underground;
in a basement or storm cellar.
If there isn't one
then choose an inside room
without windows.

Crouch under something solid,
or get into a bath.
Protect yourself
with pillows, blankets or a duvet.
You need something soft.
Never stay in a car or mobile home.

# 9 Tornado Damage

Most tornadoes are weak.
They only last a few minutes.

A few cause major damage.
Winds reach up to 300 mph.
Leaves and bark are stripped off trees.
A street of houses becomes
a pile of rubbish.

Roofs are ripped off houses.
Mobile homes are picked up
and carried by the wind.
Trucks are turned over.
Cars are swept up
and smashed into buildings.

Some tornadoes cause major damage.

Animals and people are picked up
and dropped miles away.
Sometimes they live.
Sometimes they die.

Rubbish is caught up
in the swirling wind.
The air is thick with flying bricks
and metal.
Mud and rock is raining down.
Winds this fast are deadly.

# 10 John's Story

This is John's story.

'The day of the tornado was a normal day.
By afternoon it was stormy.
News reports told us what to expect.
There was a tornado warning.
The sirens went off.

I picked up the kids
and put them in the bath.
My wife got into the bath.
I put a mattress on top
and lay on it.

There was a roaring sound.
There was this rushing air all around.
I hung on to the mattress.
No chance.
The wind picked me up
and flung me 30 feet.
There was no wall left to stop me.

A plank of wood was pushed
right through my upper arm.

Gas and water were leaking everywhere.
I looked around.
Unbelievable.

I had six apple trees
in the garden.
Not a leaf was left.
The bark was stripped off.
A smashed up truck
was in the middle of my garden.

My family was safe.
My arm is not good.
The bone was smashed.
But I'm lucky to be alive.
Many people died that day.

The warning saved my life.
It saved my family's life
and many more.

Six months after the tornado,
I still have nightmares.
But the town pulled together.
We cleaned up.
We cried together.
We helped each other.
I'm building a new house.
This one has a storm cellar.'

# 11  Finding Out More

*Twister* is a film about a tornado.
It gives an idea of what it's like.
You can get it on video.

**The Internet**
Type in tornadoes and search the net.
There are reports of recent tornadoes.
There are reports from chasers.
There are facts on tornadoes.

http://www.geocities.com/-1storm/facts.htm